You Can Transform Your Life

GO DEEPER
Workbook

Darity Wesley

Melissa Morgan

Paula Wansley

Modern Day
ORACLE

Modern Day Oracle™ Wisdom Teaching Series

Companion to Book 1

You Can Transform Your Life ~ Go Deeper © 2017 Darity Wesley

Modern Day Oracle™ © 2017 Darity Wesley

Cover Design: Paula Wansley

Symbol Illustrations: Paula Wansley

Visit our website at www.DarityWesley.com

Wesley, Darity
    You Can Transform Your Life ~ Go Deeper / Darity Wesley – 1st edition 2017

Published by Lotus Wisdom Publishing

ISBN 978-0-9995425-1-4

Lotus Wisdom
Publishing

This workbook is dedicated to YOU,
for having the courage to go deeper, to transform,
to step more fully into who you really are

Also by Darity Wesley

You Can Transform Your Life

<u>Featured Author</u>

The Word Search Oracle

21 Flavors of Fulfillment

Free yourself from what is holding you back!
Be who you truly are!

TABLE OF CONTENTS

Go Deeper Workbook

INTRODUCTION
HOW TO USE THIS BOOK

Welcome. Welcome. Welcome to the *You Can Transform Your Life ~ Go Deeper* workbook! This workbook is designed to accompany the book *You Can Transform Your Life*, to enable a more thorough journey of self-discovery and awareness. There are practical aids, guides, questions, exercises and chances to journal all created to help make your inner exploration as profound and meaningful as possible. Opportunities to really dive deep.

Can you really transform your life? In a week, in a month, in a year? Absolutely. Yes you can! Transformation is part of being human. We all grow and change and evolve. How much, when and where are all matters of personal choice. Just like we are what we eat, we are the results of the work we put into ourselves. Small, incremental changes applied regularly can yield huge and soul satisfying results.

Concepts, practices, insights, ideas, all of these are puzzle pieces to help create a whole ... a whole and happy thriving person, a whole and happy thriving world. We are moving into Unity Consciousness, a feeling of Oneness with All That Is. Or we are not. The choice is up to each of us. Every day. Every moment. Change is not only possible, it is inevitable. Applying these tools, practices and concepts helps. They are designed to ease the transition for us all.

You Can Transform Your Life is set up as a year-long process, a 52-week program with a message for each week. The *Go Deeper* workbook is created with the same organizational guidelines. However, you can use all the tools in any manner that works best for you. Skip around or work through it from start to finish or mix and match. Whatever way inspires you is just perfect.

Inner work is very personal. We all respond to things differently, grow at different paces and need more or less time with various topics. Customize this workbook to your heart's content. Respond to the self-discovery questions in the order they are written or move them around. Do exercises as written or modify them at your pleasure. Skip them if you so choose. You might even be inspired to create your own exercises or sets of questions. Feel free to copy over the symbols or mantras that you created from *You Can Transform Your Life* to further solidify their power. Or, create new ones! Personalize this workbook so it works for you!

The beauty of the whole process is to let your intuition guide you. It will take you to exactly where you need to be, looking at exactly what you need to look at, at exactly the right time. Watch for the synchronicity; it will be there. Take that as confirmation that you are doing fine and fabulous.

When answering questions, it is sometimes nice to use a couple of different approaches or combine them. The first is the Quick Approach which is to just scribble down whatever comes to mind very quickly. Don't judge it. Don't think about it. Don't let your mind get ahold of it. It doesn't have to make sense, or even be obviously on topic. The other would be the Considered Approach which is to consider carefully and deeply, perhaps even meditate upon it, to really think about and ponder your answers, for a minute or two, or even over the course of a few days or weeks.

For example: Fearlessness. What am I afraid of? The Quick Approach might be something like, "spiders, heights, being broke, dying, dark alleys late at night, losing someone I care about." The Considered Approach might be like, "What am I really afraid of? Hmmmm. Being lonely, dying alone, being ostracized from my family or friends if I change, failure, success, never being good enough, making a mistake, speaking my truth." Both ways of responding have immense value for us in the process of transforming our lives.

Again, and always, let your intuition and cosmic help team of guides and angels assist you on what approach to take for each topic, practice or exercise. (For more information on how to tune in to your cosmic help, see the exercise on page 56.) Sometimes it is helpful to use a combination of approaches on the same Oracle. In other words, first write what pops into your head, and then later add to it after deeper contemplation. How deep do you want to go? It's up to you. Another step on the transformation journey!

We live in exciting times. Change is in the air and on the horizon. The tools, principles and practices described in *You Can Transform Your Life* are signposts designed to help you navigate these changing times and facilitate your journey to your own beautiful True Authentic Self. The *You Can Transform Your Life ~ Go Deeper* workbook gives you a chance to go deeper, to really search within and find those golden nuggets we all harbor inside, sometimes unknown even to ourselves. It is truly a courageous act to look, see and explore our deepest selves. Your process of transformation is already well begun, and is absolutely and fully supported.

Stay open to the guidance coming from within. As you read the Oracle words, listen also for your own. As you answer the workbook questions or do the exercises or contemplate, know that there is grace and love and infinite help available at all times. Even if you don't feel it yet, know that you are in the right place, at the right time, doing the right thing. Taking the time to explore these thought-provoking questions and exercises from the depths of your spirit will lead you home. To yourself.

Enjoy the journey!

THE PROCESS OF SELF-DISCOVERY
WHAT COMES UP?

An important part of the *Go Deeper* process is self-inquiry. Throughout this workbook you will be asked many questions designed to help guide you on a deep and meaningful journey of self-exploration and self-discovery. These questions are designed to help stimulate thoughts and feelings that may lie below the surface of your daily consciousness, like the fiery, molten magma below a volcano's surface. Thoughts, beliefs, conditioning and feelings need to be explored to see if they are still real for you, to see if they still work, to see if they still represent what you truly and currently believe.

To set the process in motion, each topic in the *Go Deeper* workbook begins by asking w*hat comes up for you* when you consider the primary theme of the Oracle message. This is a very open-ended question and refers to anything and everything that might come up in the moment. It includes all thoughts and feelings that arise. It could be dreams, images, anxieties, visions, fears, pain, anger or frustrations. It could also be memories that have haunted you like old grief, guilt, sorrow, shame or sadness. It could also be silliness, a face, words of a loved one, an experience you just had, a movie you just saw or a mish-mash of everything. Or, sometimes, a whole lot of nothing! Whatever comes up, whatever you experience, is what it is supposed to be. Don't judge it. Don't attach to it. Just discern and observe what comes up. Why? Because *that* is what is important. Whatever comes up for you, as you respond to the questions contained in this *Go Deeper* workbook, is your treasure trove of self-discovery.

Transforming our lives, or learning more about ourselves, is a process. The things that keep us stuck, right where we are, are often parts of what is called *our shadow side.* That contains our fears, our insecurities or those parts of ourselves we all want to remain permanently hidden. Your responses to the *Go Deeper* workbook questions will help open the doors. They will let the light in. They will allow the inner volcano to erupt, revealing the deeply hidden parts of your own self-identity. All that old hidden shame and fear and doubt and denial can have its moment in the sun. Opportunities for healing will appear. What happens next can be really extraordinary. Freedom. And release. Sometimes just giving ourselves permission to open the door a crack allows us to breathe. It gives us a chance to forgive ourselves and others. It gives us a chance to heal and change. To transform.

The bottom line is that transformation is work. In the midst of it many of us feel exposed, vulnerable and scared. We wonder if anyone else has felt these feelings or questioned their sanity, or ... thought that maybe running away or hiding under the bed or tossing this book out the window is, absolutely, the best option. Well, don't!

What you experience is actually the way the process WORKS!! The fact that you want to run away or hide under the bed or toss the book out the window is a good sign. Why? Because it means you are getting down into the nitty gritty. You are getting down to the stuff that has held you up. The stuff that has kept you from your joy. Do keep going. Do hang in there. You are DOING the work, which is what it will take to transform your life.

Sometimes doing the work is hard. You might even feel the need to cry along the way or yell or scream out loud. That's ok. Allow yourself to express whatever feelings arise. Sometimes it is uncomfortable, yet that is where release and change are found. We don't stay there. You might be very surprised at how good you can feel. Our loads tend to lighten as we allow ourselves to grow and change.

Therefore, be easy with yourself. Move at a pace that allows you to gently unwind. Be kind, loving and compassionate with yourself throughout the entire process. Acknowledge your courage. Celebrate your successes. Be good to yourself along the way. You deserve it!

Remember, no matter how isolated you might feel, you are not alone in this process. Your angels and guides, and your very own inner wisdom and guidance, are available to help and support you each and every step of the way. Integrating this guidance into daily reality helps so much! It doesn't even have to be named or identified. Just let it in. Allow it. Feel it. Trust it. It will always be there for you, and can help immensely with the Go *Deeper* process and the journey of transformation.

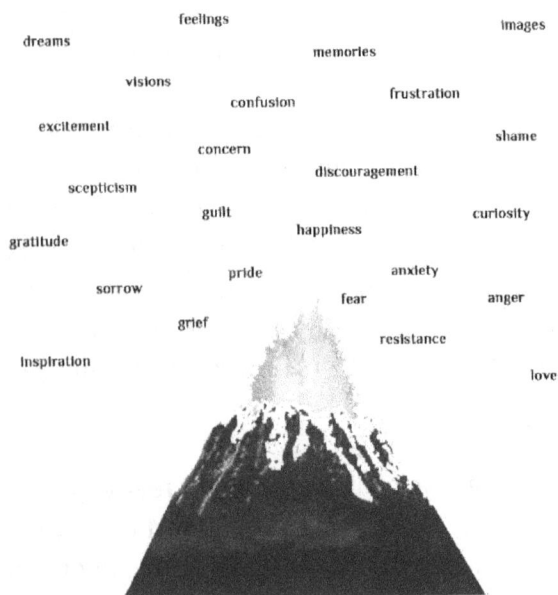

Trust that whatever erupts from your inner volcano, whatever comes up in response to the *Go Deeper* questions, will guide you to exactly where you need to go. It will serve as a guiding light ... revealing, exposing and illuminating your inner landscape.

Have Trust and Courage.

Stay open to guidance from within.

Do your best and love yourself for it.

Know, at the heart level, that All Is Well.

ALL IS WELL

One of the deep spiritual truths that is a foundation in *You Can Transform Your Life,* and here in the *Go Deeper* workbook, is the concept that All Is Well. This can seem completely confusing. Why? On one hand, we can feel the resonance that this IS a deep spiritual truth. On the other hand, how can All be Well when our lives feel like we're on a roller coaster ride? Like so many of those deep spiritual truths, it is all a matter of perspective. From the point of view of Divine Essence *All Is Well All the Time* in every circumstance, no matter how challenging it is for our human self along for the ride. What an adventure!

The wonderful thing about deep spiritual truths is that we can feel them being true even if our minds want to argue it with us. This is one the mind LOVES to argue with, presenting all kinds of proof positive evidence that not only is all not really well, all is pretty well messed up and we had better do something about it ... but what? An incredible paradox, eh?

Embracing the concept that All Is Well is really remarkably helpful. Not just in surviving everyday life, but in thriving. When things are difficult, we can remind ourselves. When they are impossible, we can chant it like a mantra. When we are at the edge, it provides us with a net. It is more than the idea of *this too shall pass.* It is an affirmation that as spiritual beings inhabiting physical bodies we are growing and changing and being challenged and surviving and even dying, and All Really Is Still Well. It's okay. We're okay at the deepest level, even when, *especially* when, we feel like we're not. We are on this planet to do more than simply exist. We have a purpose here. It is ours to discover and express. Who we REALLY are already knows deeply that All Is Well.

Embracing the concept, the truth that All Is Well, is a game changer. As we grow and change and trust God, Spirit, the Universe, All That Is, or whatever we call such energies, it allows us to view and experience adversity in a different way. It allows us to regulate our emotional responses. We really don't have to react to someone who dangerously cuts us off on the highway when we acknowledge that All Is Well. It also causes a deepening of trust within. It allows us to breathe. It allows us to listen for and trust our guides and angels, and the intuition that comes from within. It encourages us to hope. It helps us to remember that we have a bigger purpose here.

All Is Well.

THE BUDDY SYSTEM
WORKING WITH OTHERS

It is true that working on transforming ourselves requires a lot of practice and work that is sometimes difficult, deep, and frightening. While it is still incredibly rewarding, for some of us, that work goes much easier and is much more fun if it is shared. Consider a transformation buddy or group of buddies. Who pops into your mind right now? Might even be someone unexpected.

A transformation buddy, or a group you trust to share with, is not necessarily where you share everything. A lot of this work is so personal and deep and healing that it happens on the inside, not the outside. However, even simply the commitment to do this together can be a nice support system. Conversations like, *What was your most difficult challenge in dealing with fearlessness? ... My boyfriend. ... Really??? ... Mine was spiders!! ... Really? You're worried about BUGS??* Another person's perspective can help bring ours into focus.

It's certainly not about judging your friend's progress, or your own, for that matter! It's about recognizing that sometimes burdens shared are burdens halved. Knowing your friend's story, or fears, can make yours easier to tell, even if you only tell it to yourself.

Then there is the support piece. Knowing that another human being is working on the same transformational process and opening to fuller consciousness makes all the difference. Someone, somewhere, is listening and sharing. I can do this!!

Bottom line, you *can* do this. Buddy or not. We all have so much support, more than we can possibly imagine. In our hearts. In our souls. Physical, non-physical, cosmic, practical everyday feet-on-the-ground support. Some days it's hard to feel it. Other days, unmistakable. All points in between. Please, go ahead and feel it now. Let it come in to your heart!

Whether you choose to call a friend and ask them to join you in the transformation process, organize a *You Can Transform Your Life* discussion group, or if you simply set out on your own, remember that help and support is always available. Right here, right now. The Universe is always supporting you every step of the way.

GO DEEPER
Workbook

1. Creating a New Way of Life

What thoughts, feelings, memories, visions, images, dreams, ideas, etc. come up for you when you consider creating a new way of life for yourself?

If you were to imagine a new way of life for yourself, what would that be like?

What parts of your life would you like to transform and why?

What specific changes would you make?

List 3 things (or more) that you feel will improve the quality of your life. (They don't have to be large, life changing steps, or they may be.)

1.

2.

3.

What do you need or want to release to facilitate the changes?

2. Fearlessness

What comes up for you when you consider stepping into being fearless?

What places in your life has fear crept in?

What 3 fears would you like to let go of right now?

1.

2.

3.

What are you most afraid of?

Are you willing to begin to let that fear go? What would help?

In what portion of your life would you most like to embrace fearlessness in?
What is most important to you?

3. Trust

What comes up for you when you consider trusting yourself or others?

How would you describe your current level of trust in yourself and others? Are you open to becoming more trusting? Explain.

What are 3 things you can do every day to help practice trust?

1.

2.

3.

Are you willing to do them? If so, write a commitment. If not, write why not now. Explore your feelings.

What challenges are you experiencing in your life that would be improved by trust?

How do you think having more trust would impact your life?

How can you help yourself build trust?

Exercise: All Is Well

For this exercise, there is space to journal on the next page.

Sit quietly for a few minutes. Breathe. Slow it down. In. Out. In. Out. Find that calm center within yourself, as best you can. Say quietly, "All Is Well." Breathe some more. Say it again, "All Is Well." Take a deep, long slow breath. "All Is Well." See if you can feel the resonance of the truth of the statement.

If you feel it, stay with it. Integrate it. If other thoughts or arguments against the concept come up, step into the next exercise below.

It's ok if you can't feel it. It may be new to you, or it may be something you have met before, but had trouble integrating. If so, do this same breathing process. Only this time write down all the things your mind is saying to refute the "All Is Well" statement.

For example, let's say that these are the things that come up:
    Oh, no it is not!
    My wife, husband, friend is dying.
    My car needs work.
    There is too much violence in the world.
    I'm broke.
    I don't like my job.
    My relationship is falling apart and I don't know what to do.

Don't spend a lot of time or ruminate, just jot down whatever rises up to the surface of your mind while you are in the breathing process. Don't edit it. If "This is stupid!" comes up, write it down. Breathe a little more. Get a drink of water. Stretch.

Sit down. Begin again. Breathe. Slow it down. Get quiet. Now say, "All Is Well," and cross out the first thing on your list. You might choose to use a pencil. Or maybe a really black marker! You choose. And repeat the process saying "All Is Well" and strike the next thing, continuing until all are crossed out. Feel it as you say it. Believe it as you say it. Say it over and over, like a mantra. Know at the highest level that, indeed, All Is Well.

Let other thoughts bubble up. Even if they are distractions from the exercise like, "I'm hungry," or "This is dumb," or "This will never work." Stick with it! Continue to explore the feelings and change each one from within to, "All Is Well. Everything is okay."

Feel free to scratch out anything that does not match the truth within you.

Congratulations! Excellent work! All Is Well.

Journal: All Is Well

Journal here your experience with the exercise All Is Well. Do it more than once. Make it a practice which will support the integration of this deep spiritual truth in your life.

4. Cornerstone

What comes up for you when you consider whether or not you have a cornerstone
for your life?

What are your core beliefs and principles? Write some here.

Have you reviewed your core beliefs and principles recently? Are they congruent with
who you are now?

Are there any new cornerstones you would like to establish for yourself?

Write some new thoughts or ideas about how you see yourself and/or how you would like to be in the world.

What steps can you take to become more solid in your sense of self and your cornerstone?

5. Determination

ORACLE MESSAGE:
*Determination means firmness of purpose
and being resolute in decisions.*

What comes up for you when you consider what determination means to you?

Are you determined? If so, how do you express it?

If not, what do you want to do to become more determined?

What ambitions do you have that are close to your heart that excite you?

What goals can you create to achieve them?

What steps would move you closer to those goals?

6. Fired

What comes up for you when you consider removing something from your life, to fire it?

Is the word *fired* a trigger for you? How so?

If so, are there other words you'd be more comfortable using instead of *fired*? Use those.

Is there something you'd like to fire yourself from? What and why?

Is there someone you'd like to fire from your life? Who and why?

What steps are you ready to take now to begin the firing process? Are you feeling any resistance?

What do you need to make yourself feel better about the concept or idea of leaving something behind?

7. Quiet

ORACLE MESSAGE:
*It is thinking and feeling and exploring and going deeper
that actually fuels our inner work.*

What comes up for you when you consider putting some quiet time in your life?

Do you have quiet time in your day now? When?

If you don't, when would you like it?

Where or how could you increase your quiet time? First thing in the morning? Last thing at night? During lunch? Travel time? An extra moment in the bathroom while washing your hands? Sunday afternoons? Monday mornings early? Late at night when you're the only one awake?

What would work for you? Describe it.

Consider creating a sacred space for yourself. Describe your ideal sacred space.

What sacred space can you create for yourself today?

A surprising number of people consider their cars to be sacred space. Do you? Just the act of declaring something sacred can be surprisingly powerful. What ordinary spaces in your life would you like to deem sacred?

8. Strategy

What comes up for you when you consider devising a strategy for your transformative practices?

What decisions, visions, aspirations are you ready to bring into your reality?

What is your strategy to put them into place?

What is a simple one you could start right now? Or at least imagine?

Devise your strategy. Break things down into very small steps. What's next?
And after that?

9. The Big Picture

What comes up for you when you consider The Big Picture?

Do you have a Big Picture? What does it look like?

Let your guides share something with your right now about your Big Picture.

Take note of what was shared or felt.

Were you surprised by the content?

Is there a small step you can take today that will help you aim in that direction?

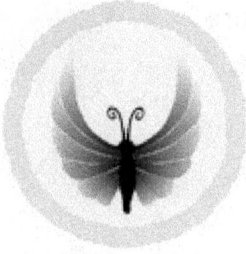

10. Uniqueness

What comes up for you when you consider that you are unique?

How does it feel? Does it feel good? Does it feel true? What are your impressions?

What do you recognize that is unique about you?

How can you express it more?

What impact do you think you or your uniqueness has on others?

What would you change about your relationship with yourself if you could change one thing, instantly, right now?

Do you feel that you are blossoming? If not, write what's holding you back. Or who? If so, write how you experience your blossoming.

What can you do to celebrate YOU and your uniqueness?

11. Who You Think You Are

What comes up for you when you think about who you *really* are?

Do you feel like you know who you *really* are?

How would you describe yourself?

Who were you taught to be?

Are you now different from who you were taught to be? If so, how?

Who are you *really*?

What 3 things could you do right now to help you become more of who you *really* are?
Do you know? Are you willing to consider it? Ask your guides for help. Write your thoughts.

1.

2.

3.

Do you have any fears or resistance to expressing more of who you *really* are? Explore.

If so, what steps can you take to feel safe to express more of who you *really* are out in
the world?

12. Vulnerabilities

What comes up for you when you consider allowing yourself to be more vulnerable?

In what areas of your life do you feel vulnerable?

What shields do you have in place to protect yourself?

How might your life change if you became more open and vulnerable?

What hopes and desires would be able to enter your life as a result?

Are you willing to become more vulnerable, or do you feel like you need to be in control? Explore.

What steps can you take to put down your shields and allow your vulnerability to show through? Are you willing?

13. Forgiveness

What comes up for you when you consider forgiving yourself or others?

What traumas or emotional scars are you still carrying from the past?

Do you feel like a victim? How much of the time? What would change that for you?

What or who have you not been able to forgive?

How has this inability to forgive affected your life?

Are you ready to forgive them? If you are, write a statement of forgiveness. Make it so.

What are some things you can do to practice forgiveness on a daily basis?

Exercise: Forgiveness

Begin by sitting in a quiet place without distractions. Follow your breath. Breathe. Slow it down. In. Out. In. Out. Let your mind do its thing and then bring your attention back to your breath.

Now, if you are in a safe place where no one can hear you, say aloud, "I am ready to forgive myself for _____" and fill in the blank with the first thing that comes up for you in that moment.

If you are not ready to do this exercise here, now, take some time to prepare yourself and come back and do it. Do it for yourself. Do it for those you want to forgive but have not allowed yourself to forgive. Do it more than once. Do it as often as you need to. This is a great exercise. Forgiveness lifts an enormous burden off of our shoulders, one we often did not even know was there.

Forgiveness puts aside resentment, indignation or anger directed at yourself or others. It is a choice to no longer engage in such feelings. These feelings might have come from something you or someone else did, maybe even a long time ago, or a perceived offense, some kind of disagreement or even a mistake by another person.

Remember that forgiveness is neutral. It is done by the heart, not the mind. It's about letting it all go. Sometimes what we know we need to forgive ourselves for doesn't make sense to the brain. Something may come up that makes your mind go, "Huh? Wait!" Go with it anyway. If your heart says, "I need to forgive myself for being in pain," just go ahead and do so. It does not have to make sense.

Sometimes what we know we need to forgive others for does not make sense to the brain either. How can you forgive THAT??! Again, go with it anyway. If your heart says "I need to forgive my mother, father, brother, sister, husband, wife for _____" just go ahead and do it. It doesn't have to make sense.

Now, state your forgiveness aloud. "I forgive myself for ... " or "I forgive X for ... "

Next imagine all the emotions, all the stuff around this topic bubbling up and out of you. Some see it as colors, some see it as rays of light, some as old black tar. Some people do not see anything visually, yet feel a sense or sensation. However you perceive whatever it is for you, let it lift up and away. Let it go. Feel the freedom. Keep breathing.

Ask your guides and angels to fill up any empty spaces that may be created with unconditional love and light. Visualize, if that is what works for you, or sit calmly, knowing that it is happening because you asked. You will know when you are done. You are free. There will be a lightness in the deepest part of your heart. Sometimes it takes time for that to show. Sometimes we have to grieve a bit. Treat yourself with loving compassion.

Ask your guides and non-physical support team for help. If old emotions come up, ask your team to facilitate their release. No more burden!

Journal your experience below and on the following pages.

I forgive myself for ...

What does your heart say about that?

What do your guides say?

What do you experience when you bubble up and out your emotions?

How do you feel when you fill empty spaces with unconditional love and light?

What did you experience or learn from doing this exercise?

Forgiveness List

What are you ready to forgive? Fill in the blanks below and make it so!

I am ready to forgive _____ for _____
_____

Statement of forgiveness: _____
_____

I am ready to forgive _____ for _____
_____

Statement of forgiveness: _____
_____

I am ready to forgive _____ for _____
_____

Statement of forgiveness: _____
_____

I am ready to forgive _____ for _____
_____

Statement of forgiveness: _____
_____

I am ready to forgive _____ for _____
_____

Statement of forgiveness: _____
_____

CONGRATULATIONS! GREAT WORK!

Journal: Forgiveness

Journal here your experience with the exercise on Forgiveness.

14. Gratitude

What comes up for you when you consider feeling grateful?

What are some of the things and people in your life that you are most grateful for?

What in your life are you NOT grateful for? What circumstances have you been resisting or complaining about?

Consider being grateful for even those circumstances. What about them can you be grateful for? How have they served you?

How did it feel when you did the starry night meditation in the book *You Can Transform Your Life*? What did you discover?

What steps can you take to make gratitude a daily practice?

Exercise: My Gratitude List

Making and keeping a *Gratitude List* is a very important exercise and spiritual practice. It can be referenced on days when you feel down or discouraged or if you feel like you aren't making any progress at all. It will be there on days when you simply need a bit of a lift, for whatever reason, or simply to add feelings of joy and gratitude to any day.

What are you grateful for? Awareness of things that we are grateful for can come to us over time. We can think of lots of them off the tops of our heads and that's great! List them here! Know that more will come to you later. As you become aware of them over the next few hours, coming days, weeks and months, write them down in the space provided. Keep your Gratitude List ongoing. Often the days they come to us are good days. Being able to remember and access those good days on tough days is part of our transformation process.

Get more paper if you need to or have a special section in your journal. Some like to dedicate an entire blank journal book to be their Gratitude Journal.

Remember to include nature, whether a favorite walk on a beautiful beach whether imaginary or not, night skies, sunrises, sunsets, animals both wild and home companions, those present or across the Rainbow Bridge. And everyday things like hot and cold running water, phones, electricity, libraries, cars, farmers, grocery stores, music, the Internet. Include people you love, those who have been kind to you, or have mentored you, family, friends, teachers, bosses, significant others. And so on.

It is also a great conversation to have with a close friend. "What's on your gratitude list?" Not only will it brighten up the day, but sharing our lists with others presents each of us with more ideas for what to add to our own lists!

Have fun making the list. Take just a moment to savor each item. Aren't we lucky? There is, truly, so much to be grateful for!

I Am Grateful For ...

_____

_____

_____

_____

_____

_____

_____

_____

_____

_____

_____

_____

_____

_____

~ I am in deep gratitude for All That Is. ~

15. Grounding

What comes up for you when you consider grounding yourself?

Do you feel grounded right now?

Can you tell when you are not grounded? How?

Can you tell when you are grounded? How?

How might being more grounded benefit your life?

What are some ways you know of to ground yourself?

Now, ask your guides for some additional ways you can use to ground yourself. Their suggestions might be unexpected. Write them down here.

What steps can you take to ground yourself on a more regular basis? Make a plan. What can you do? When would you do it? What would be a good time? Day or night?

16. Now

What comes up for you when you consider bringing yourself into the present moment?

What does NOW feel like to you, in a general sense? How would you describe it?

Do you feel that you live mostly in the present? What aspects of your past show up the most in the present?

Do you tend to live in the past? The future? Both?

Take a moment, right now, to be present. Fully present, right here, right now. How does it feel?

Is it easy for you to be fully present? What pulls you away?

What easy steps can you take to remind yourself to return to the NOW?

17. Balance

What comes up for you when you think about whether you are in a balanced state of being?

How would you describe your *old self*?

How would you describe the *new self* you are becoming, or want to become?

What is the current state of your internal balance? Write about it here.

What types of situations throw you off balance?

What methods do you use to restore equilibrium?

Are you able to remain spiritually detached when handling life's challenges and dramas?

Do you have equal balance between involvement in the material world and a spiritual detachment from it? Describe.

In what ways are you being guided by your angels, spirit guides and your own soul?

What types of messages have you been receiving about being balanced?

What steps can you take to deepen and improve your inner balance?

18. Study & Support

What comes up for you when you consider studying and supporting yourself?

How do you feel about learning something new?

Do you consider yourself curious? Spiritually? Intellectually? In what ways are you curious?

What subjects or new perspectives would you be interested in learning about?

What skills would you like to develop at some point, now or in the future?

Are there any issues around learning for you? What are they?

Do you recognize yourself as a power for change? In what ways?

What steps can you take to expand your knowledge level or experience, whether personal, professional or spiritual?

19. Surrender

What comes up for you when you think about surrendering?

What does surrender mean to you?

Do you have a reaction/response to the word itself? What is it? Do you consider it positive? Negative? Neutral? Scary? A strength? A weakness? Write it here.

Take a moment to connect with the Divine Love that is buried deep within you. Fill yourself with it. What does that love feel like? What comes up for you?

What do you perceive as your life's purpose right now?

Are you willing to consider that maybe it has evolved? That you now have another purpose that is more aligned with your emerging self? What might that be? Ask your guides for help.

What are you holding onto, in each category below, that no longer serves you?

Old thinking patterns ...

Old resentments ...

Old worn-out relationships ...

Old beliefs ...

Old habits ...

Old places and things ...

Old ideas about who you are or who you want to be ...

Anything else that no longer serves you ...

What steps can you take to surrender it all?

20. The Inner Voice

ORACLE MESSAGE:
Take the time to quiet the mind and listen with your heart.

What comes up for you when you consider connecting with and listening to your inner voice?

What relationship do you have with your inner voice? Is it part of your daily life?

What steps can you take to deepen that relationship?

How do you feel when you listen to your inner voice?

Does your inner voice have a particular sound or tone? Describe it.

How can you tell it from your thoughts? Is there something special about your inner voice?

Take a moment right now to stop the mind and listen. Quiet your mind and listen with your heart. What is that voice telling you right now? Can you hear it? Do you trust it? Write your experience. (If you heard nothing, try again, several times a day until you hear it. You will!)

What are some of the recent promptings of your inner voice?

Say right now, aloud, "I will trust my inner voice."

What comes up for you when you say that? Will you/Can you do it?

Exercise: Tuning In

How we increase the connection we have to our inner voice, our intuition, our non-physical support team is different for everyone. If your intuitive connection is strong and alive and well, and you speak with your angels and guides daily, then you definitely know how to "tune in." If this is a new process for you, or if you wish to deepen your connection even further, here is a process to help.

Find a place and a time where you can relax, turn off the phone and be alone without any distractions. Sit or lie comfortably and begin to slow your breathing. Now, follow your breath with your attention. No need for a particular breathing style; it can be distracting to make yourself breathe a certain way. Just feel your lungs fill, then empty. Most people's brains turn on at this point and start presenting all the other things you could be doing, errands to run, kids to pick up, the grocery list ... calmly bring your attention back to your breath each time your mind wanders. Don't argue with your mind; it doesn't help. Just continue to bring your focus back to your breath ... gently.

Say aloud or silently to yourself, "I would like to contact my guides." If you are working on intuition, you can use a different phrase such as "I would like to deepen my intuition." State your intention. Be prepared for parts of your mind to have a variety of responses to this. Some people have an internal jeering section. Go back to focusing on your breath and state your intention again, "I would like to contact my guides." Let the brain have its reaction and state calmly, once again, "I would like to contact my guides." Then focus again on your breath, and listen. Listen within.

It depends on where you are internally as to what happens next. Some people may get a quiet, "Yes," coming from that still, quiet voice within. Some people may see elaborate details in Technicolor, or clearly hear the sound of their guides speaking. Most of us start small and quiet and maybe even a bit confused and questioning. "Did I actually hear anything? Was that a yes?" It's ok if you don't hear, feel or see anything. Trust yourself. Trust the process. Know that something is happening, even if it doesn't seem like it.

Imagine if you wanted to be an opera singer, but had never sung in public before. Step one is not going to be stepping out on the stage in a massive performance hall. Step one would be singing, using your voice frequently, maybe getting some lessons or advice. You'd build up to that performance hall with daily practice and vocal exercise. Intuition and communication with your non-physical support team works the same way. The first thing is to decide you want to. Then to state your intention out loud, "I want this! I want to be in touch with my guides! I want to be able to access my intuition!" And then grow it. A little at a time. Step-by-step. Daily, if possible, but don't judge yourself if it's not. When and as you can. Lots of us get communication at unexpected times, like driving to work, while taking a shower or just before falling asleep. So, once you've stated your intent, be open to receiving communication any time of the day or night.

So, you've been practicing paying attention to your breath, quieting your mind, stating your intention and listening. Believe it or not, that's the protocol. That's all there is to do. Some people use guided imagery, some use sound and/or drumming, some go for overt meditation. Many pray. Even if it doesn't seem like it's working, know that it is.

It's very important to know that *tuning in* always accesses the highest and best. That is where your trust comes in. The tone is always loving, supportive, kind and understanding. If you perceive things that sound like noise or are in any way negative, go back to following your breath and go deeper. Ask for help. Sometimes our monkey minds like to play tricks. Once you have heard or felt the voice of your own intuition, or contacted your guides, it is unmistakable. You and your heart will always recognize and know the quality of that inner voice from then on. Trust yourself.

When contact is established, it's always nice to be polite. Please and thank you, especially when we are asking for help, whether with specific challenges or general help. Most people feel a solid wave of love when they are in contact with their guides. It's nice to acknowledge their help, love, kindness, compassion and caring by sending our own waves of love back to them. But only if it feels right to you. Intuition and communication with guides is intensely personal. Handle it in the way that feels just right to you. And if you have doubts or questions, feel free to ask your guides! They tend to be quite straightforward in their responses and may even show a little bit (or a lot!) of personality. They LIKE to help and, just like any other being, they enjoy being acknowledged. Follow your heart. You'll know exactly what to say or do, when to do it and how.

Being able to consciously *tune in* to and connect with your inner guidance is one of the most extraordinary and beneficial abilities you can develop along the spiritual path. All it takes is intention, practice, listening and trust. Ultimately it becomes part of your daily experience. That we know we are guided, loved and supported all along the way makes all the difference!

Journal: Tuning In

Journal your experience of *tuning in*, whatever it may be. Record any messages or inspiration that you received. Don't worry if the first few sessions are blanks; you'll get there! Keep at it!

Journal: Tuning In

21. Appreciation

What comes up for you when you think about consciously awakening feelings of appreciation?

Name 3 (or more) things that you truly appreciate in your life.

1.

2.

3.

Name 3 (or more) people that you truly appreciate in your life.

1.

2.

3.

Do you feel appreciated by others? If so, how? If not, why?

What is the difference between gratitude and appreciation?

What are some examples from your own life?

How do you feel when you appreciate things or people?

How do you feel when you are appreciated by others?

Exercise: Appreciation

For our exercise in appreciation, Melissa Morgan shares a personal story that changed her life in a big way. She has a lifelong friend who shared her interest in spirituality and philosophy. When they were young, somewhere in their 20s, they decided to try an experiment with appreciation. They had noticed, especially in their careers, but also in their personal lives, that people don't express a lot of appreciation for each other. At work, after a large project's completion, instead of praise and appreciation, it was on to the next thing.

They decided to experiment. They used each other as test subjects and, evidently, got pretty silly about the whole thing. How much appreciation was too much? Is there a ceiling? And so they complimented each other and acknowledged each other's hard work and kept upping the ante more and more. They got up to saying to each other, "Vast waves of appreciation are crashing upon your shores." And they found that those vast waves felt pretty good. They then realized that there was no ceiling, no limit on how much appreciation one can take. Sincere appreciation, honestly expressed, means the world. And, you know what? We are all hungry for it. It does feel so good to be seen and appreciated.

So, the exercise here is to think about appreciation in your own life. Both giving and receiving. Was there one boss or friend or teacher who was appreciative? Or who saw a talent in you that you may not have even seen in yourself? Who supported you? Who supports you now? We would all do just about anything for a person that appreciates us, right? It feels like it is so rare for people to truly see and acknowledge our hard work and efforts, that when anyone does, it is a red letter day and a cause for celebration. And, sometimes, shock.

Think now about becoming one of those people who notices, acknowledges and appreciates. Whether it is a member of your household making coffee in the morning or someone who put the extra effort in at work or at home or at the grocery store. A simple: "Good job!!" "Excellent work!!" or "I'm so proud of you!!" Those words feel so good! Take the time to warm the hearts of others.

The key with appreciation is to never speak superficially, falsely or even lie about what you are feeling. Humans can truly intuit sincerity. So, be sincere in your appreciation. There is so much beauty to acknowledge and see and celebrate shining out from people. This is part of being our True Authentic Selves and consciously living in the New Reality. We see and notice and acknowledge the amazingness of people and even ourselves!

Vast waves of appreciation are crashing upon your shores! Allow it in! Keep up the good work! Excellent job! I am so very proud of you, and touched by your efforts here. What you are doing takes courage.

Journal: Appreciation

Make a list of people you appreciate, and the steps you would like to take to acknowledge them. Journal your ideas on how you can express more appreciation in your life.

_____

_____

_____

_____

_____

_____

_____

_____

_____

_____

_____

_____

_____

_____

_____

22. Adventure

What comes up for you when you think about life being an adventure?

Do you feel like you have adventure in your life? If yes, write down what. If no, how can you bring adventure in?

What types of adventure would you like to experience?

Plan an adventure right now. Doesn't have to be big or dramatic. Something doable, that you can commit to in this moment. What will you commit to doing?

Describe it.

Have you stopped enjoying the journey? If so, why? If not, what aspects of your life bring you the most enjoyment?

Are you ready to have more of a sense of adventure about your life?

What steps can you take to renew or expand your sense of adventure?

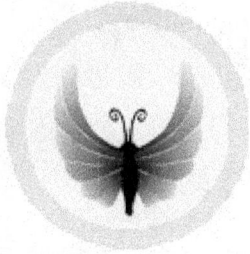

23. Fluidity

What comes up for you when you think about being fluid? Is it scary? Exciting?

Do you feel Divine energy flowing through you right now?

If so, how do you experience it?

If not, what do you think would help you to feel it? (Ask your guides for help if answers don't flow right away.)

In what areas of your life do you need to be more fluid? What challenges are you facing that keep you stuck?

Create or choose a personal mantra to remind yourself to be more fluid, for use in challenging times or when things don't go as planned. (Darity's favorite mantra for fluidity is to say, *I don't mind what happens*. Another popular mantra is, *It is what it is*.)

Write your own personal mantra for fluidity here:

What steps you can take to increase your fluidity in life?

24. Play

What comes up for you when you consider taking some time to play in your life?

What are your favorite ways to play? What is play time for you?

What are some of your fantasies? How can you play them out, even if only in your imagination or through art?

What areas of your life feel the most somber and serious?

In what ways can your inner kid help lighten up those areas, even if just for a moment?

How can you re-create yourself with play time? How can you use your inner child to enjoy life more?

What are some small things could you do every day that would feel like play? What would bring you tidbits of great pleasure and fun?

What could you do or plan right now that would be fun? Do it! Plan it!

Schedule in some play time! Or engage in FUN spontaneously!

25. Expression

What comes up for you when you think about honestly expressing yourself?

In what situations do you fully express yourself, fearlessly?

In what situations do you limit or hold yourself back from truly being yourself? Why?

How often do you modify your behavior because you worry what others might think?

Do you limit expression of your True Self on a regular basis? What are some examples?

What are some steps you can take to more fully express your True Self?

What does your True Self feel like? What does it feel like when you are expressing it?

Express your True Self right here, right now. You don't have to go on and on, though you can. What is important for you to express in this moment? Write it here.

Awesome!!! Great job!! Don't judge yourself or your expression. Just let it be. The wisdom of it may come to you in pieces, over time. Congratulate yourself for having the courage to do it at all! Go you!!

26. Kindness

What comes up for you when you consider practicing kindness every day?

Do you consider yourself to be a kind person? What are some examples of your kindness?

What types of situations bring out your kindness? How does it make you feel?

Celebrate yourself in your kindness!

What are some examples of when others have been kind to you? How did it make you feel to be treated that way?

Are you kind to yourself? In what ways?

In what ways are you not very kind to yourself?

What steps can you take to be more kind to yourself?

Who could benefit from your kindness in the next 24 hours? What act of kindness can you offer them?

Be kind to yourself no matter what!

Exercise: Celebrate Your Progress!

If you are doing this process week-by-week, you have reached the halfway point and it's time to celebrate YOU! Congratulations!

Transformation work is very interesting. When we spend the time to look deep within we can find surprising things. Sometimes wonderful and marvelous. Sometimes difficult. Sometimes sad. Sometimes joyful. The fact that we keep going even when it is difficult is a testament to our courage and determination. No one, even those who know you best, may realize how hard you are working at this or the challenges you have overcome. So, it's time for you to celebrate your progress so far!

GO YOU!!! WOO HOO!!!
AMAZING!!! AWESOME JOB!!!
YOU ARE EXTRAORDINARY!!!
YOU ARE WONDERFUL!!!

Just like everything else, people celebrate in a variety of ways. I know some people who have created a celebration dance. Every time they integrate a practice, overcome a fear, connect with something special, there's their own victory dance and they are stepping it out around their living room. Some celebrate with a pot of their favorite tea or a special dessert. Some call a good friend who lives far away and share. Some just quietly acknowledge the changes they have made and make notes in their journal. Some enjoy ceremonies.

Whatever way you like to celebrate, come up with something special that acknowledges your hard work and reminds you of the rewards. This doesn't have to be a week-long party, though it can be if you have the time and the inclination! Some little ritual, song, dance, sage, a special treat, a bubble bath, reach out to a friend or family member, something.

If you do choose to share your progress with someone else, be sure to choose your people wisely. Find folks who are willing to celebrate you with you and that you know will genuinely support you. This isn't the time for naysayers. Save your skeptics for other discussions.

However you choose to celebrate, find a way that is comforting and meaningful to you, and then do it. Frequently! You deserve it!

This week I want to celebrate myself for ...

I've made a lot of progress in ...

I still have more to do, but I am excited about the changes so far in ...

Fill in the blank: I love how adding _____ has improved the quality of my life!

I'm very excited about ...

I'm proud of myself for ...

I'm thrilled to be able to ...

Ways that I can celebrate ME and my progress ...

WOO HOO HOO!!! GO YOU!!! FABULOUS JOB!!! YOU ARE TRANSFORMING!!! YAY!!!
CONGRATULATIONS!!! KEEP UP THE GOOD WORK!!!

27. Laughter

What comes up for you when you think about laughing?

What are some things that make you laugh?

Describe the role of laughter in your life. Is it a big part of your life? Do you laugh a lot? A little? At all? Do you love to laugh? Do you seek out opportunities to laugh?

Do you love your laugh? Why or why not?

Research time! Notice over the next week or so every time you become amused. Notice what makes you laugh. See if you can make it even more funny or enjoy it more.

Write about your experience here.

Draw a picture here, or write a funny joke, that will make you laugh every time you see it.

What steps can you take to add more laughter to your life?

LOL! How's it feel?

28. Unconditional Love

What comes up for you for when you consider what unconditional love is?

What does unconditional love feel like to you? Or how would you imagine that it would feel?

Would you be willing to love something or someone unconditionally? Are you willing to practice it? If so, what would be your first steps?

What are the most common criticisms you have about yourself?

How can you transform those critical thought patterns? What steps can you take to release them? What new thoughts can you replace them with?

Are you willing to unconditionally love yourself? If so, what would be your first steps? (This one takes work for many of us. Don't worry. You'll get there! Ask your guides for help.)

29. Dignity

> **ORACLE MESSAGE:**
> *Each human being is a spark of Divine Energy expressing itself.*

What comes up for you when you contemplate the real meaning of dignity?

Do you have a sense of your own dignity? Describe it.

What can you do to increase your sense of dignity?

What is the difference between dignity and respect? What are some examples from your own life?

List at least 3 things about yourself that are worthy of dignity.

1.

2.

3.

List at least 3 things about yourself that are of significant value to this world.

1.

2.

3.

List at least 3 things about yourself that are lovable.

1.

2.

3.

What are some examples of dignity that you recognize in others?

What are some ways that you can treat yourself and others with more dignity?

30. Healing

What comes up for you when you consider tapping into healing energies?

Bring in some healing energy, right here, right now. Connect with it. Explore it.

Do you feel any resistance?

How does it feel? Describe it. Make note of any guidance that you receive.

What would you like to heal within yourself ... physical, emotional, mental, whatever calls out to you?

Do you believe you can use your own healing energy to heal it? Would you be willing to give it a try? Yes? Aren't you awesome?! Describe your experience.

Connect with and describe the healing energy within you. What can you do with it? How can you use it?

Do you believe you are a healer? What are your thoughts about that? What does your inner voice say?

What steps can you take to increase your awareness of the healing energy within, or the belief that you are a healer (if you want to)?

31. Illusion

What comes up for you when you consider this all being an illusion?

Open yourself to the idea and ask your guides to support you in stepping up to a new level of understanding the illusion. Write down what comes through here.

Do you feel any resistance to awakening from a false perception of reality? To seeing beyond the illusion? What do you fear?

What do you see as deeply real?

What do you know for sure is an illusion?

Are there areas of your life where you are only seeing what you want to see?

What do you think would make it easier to pierce the veil?

What steps can you take to open your eyes even more, to dive more fully into the unknown?

32. Inherent Wisdom

What comes up for you when you think about tapping into your inherent wisdom?

What is your inherent wisdom telling you right now? Tap into it. If you receive a message or even a feeling, write it down or describe it here.

Did you experience any resistance when listening for your inner wisdom?

Do you tend to function mostly from your heart center or from your mind? Or both?

Are you able to consciously drop from your mind into your heart center? To shift?

What spiritual practice can you use as a reminder to drop from the mind into the heart? Trust your inherent wisdom. Explore some ideas for yourself.

Do you feel you have the ability to see to the bottom of things? How's that feel? What is an example?

How can you make that stronger or enhance it? How can you use your inherent wisdom to more clearly see the truth of things?

33. Leap of Faith

What comes up for you when you think about taking a leap of faith? (Consider using *leap of trust*, or another term of your choice, if a different word resonates more with you.)

What changes have you been pondering that would require a leap? What have you been wanting to do but have been holding yourself back?

What do you fear?

Describe a time when you faced your fears. Describe the experience. How did it feel?

Is there something you have wanted to say or express that you have been hesitant about saying? If so, what is it?

Is there something you want to experience or be that you have been resistant to explore? If so, what is it?

What steps can you take to overcome at least one of your fears?

Ask your guides to reveal something you need to know right now. Listen with your heart. What are they telling you?

Exercise: My Leap of Faith

The following exercise can support you in coming up with your own personal *Leap of Faith*.

Again, as with most of these practices, start by making sure that you are in a quiet space without distractions and won't be interrupted. Begin by relaxing and breathing. Follow your breath. Slow everything down and tune in to your deep inner guidance. Keep breathing and while relaxing and breathing deeply, make a commitment to change. Say it to yourself. "I am committed to change." Now, connect with your internal guidance and ask if it is time for you to take a specific leap of faith or leap of trust with regard to a particular person or situation in your life. Or, you can begin with a blank slate, and simply ask "What would be the most beneficial change for me to make in my life right now?" Stay with it. Keep breathing slowly. Keep listening to the still small voice within and then explore the following questions for yourself.

What areas of your life came up regarding taking a leap?

What information did you receive? What comes up?

How do you feel about the information that you received?

Are you ready to make the change? Let's explore ...

What is this change you want to make in your life right now?

What has been holding you back from making this change?

What is now pushing you forward?

What would make it easier to take the leap?

What is making it harder?

What are you afraid of?

What will happen if you do it anyway, take the leap, fears and all?

What will be the result if you never take the leap?

Is it worth taking the leap?

Are you ready now to do it?

If so, complete the following sentences to solidify your commitment:

I am taking the leap of faith to _____

_____

I am committed to changing this for myself now because _____

_____

This change will benefit me by _____

_____

I release my fear of _____

_____

It is my hope that this change will _____

_____

MY LEAP OF FAITH

Remember, a leap of faith (or leap of trust) can be dramatic or subtle, external or inward. You can begin with a particular spiritual practice, or simply by approaching the issue or person with greater honesty and authenticity. You can also make bold and dramatic changes, if that is what feels right for you. Only you know what is best for you.

These are the changes I will make and the steps I will follow:

_____

_____

_____

_____

_____

Journal: My Leap of Faith

Take the time to record your experience, whatever it may be. Record any messages or inspiration that you received.

_____

_____

_____

_____

_____

_____

_____

_____

_____

_____

_____

_____

_____

_____

_____

_____

_____

34. Introspection

ORACLE MESSAGE:
*Introspection is the act of looking within,
in a deep and non-judgmental manner.*

What comes up for you when you consider looking within yourself?

In what ways are you introspective? In what areas of your life?

Do you find that your introspection is often judgmental? If so, what steps can you take to shift that judgment to something more beneficial?

Do the values, beliefs and attitudes you were raised with still work for you? Write which ones yes and which ones no.

Observe and write down how some of your personality traits impact how you think about yourself.

Congratulations on your shifts and progress! That you have chosen something consciously is awesome! Keep up the good work! All your hard work is paying off! Go within and get to know the *real* you. You are way more amazing than you imagine!

35. Abandonment

What comes up for you when you think about what abandonment means here?

Is there someone or something it is time for you to abandon? If so, what? Who?

Can you walk away and not feel guilty? Write why or why not.

Many of us have negative associations with the idea of abandonment. Consider this:
I am ready to abandon my fear of ... losing my job, becoming homeless, being alone, etc.

Write your answers here.

I am ready to abandon my fear of ...

I want ...

I need ...

I choose ...

I let go of ...

I am now free from ...

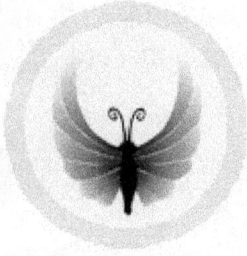

36. Acceptance

What comes up for you when you consider releasing resistance and stepping into acceptance?

What things in and about your life have you not been able to accept?

What things or people in and about your life cause you to feel resistance?

How does it feel when you resist what IS?

What can you do to release that resistance, to bring yourself into a state of acceptance?

What comes up when you consider that everything that happens in life is here for our experience?

Describe some ways in which you could use acceptance as a spiritual practice.

37. Caution

What comes up for you when you think about the need to be cautious?

Does the word caution itself have a charge for you? What?

Can you feel that All Is Well? Can you balance the discernment of caution with knowing All Is Well? Express how that feels.

Describe a time when you jumped to conclusions or made inaccurate assumptions. Why do you think that happened?

What steps can you take to be more aware, to bring yourself into the present moment, before making assumptions?

Ask your guides if there is any person, place or thing in your world right now that you need to be cautious of. What do they say?

38. Perceptiveness

What comes up for you when you consider heightening your perceptiveness?

Do you feel you are perceptive? If so, how? If not, why?

Do you rely on your intuition? If so, how? If not, why?

What are some examples of your intuitive perception?

Have your intuitive skills grown? In what way?

Do you feel part of Unity Consciousness? Oneness? Write what it feels like.

If not feeling it yet, what could you do to bring it in more? It's ok if you don't have answers. Ask your guides. Write what you receive.

Consider something you have perceived today that you might have missed, ignored or not noticed a year ago. Acknowledge your growth.

How has your perception changed?

Celebrate your progress! Write something celebratory about your perceptiveness:

39. Change

What comes up for you when you think about all the changes going on?

Do you embrace change? In what ways? In what areas of your life?

Do you resist change? In what ways? In what areas of your life?

Do you enjoy initiating change in your life, or do you tend to resist change?

How would you describe your relationship to change? Is it scary? Exciting? Intimidating? Fun? Uncomfortable? All of the above?

What do you personally want to change? In your life? In your experience? Ask your guides for help.

Relax. Open. Receive. All Is Well. Release self-judgment.

Exercise: Perception and Change

Are you aware that you can change how you feel about what is happening around you? Do you know that your response is what dictates your experience, not what other people do? Do you feel at sea with all the changes happening in the outer world now? The world of duality? It is all about perception. Let's explore ...

Start by relaxing and breathing, slowing everything down. Bring in, as much as you can, the deep inner sense that All Is Well. (If finding that feeling is a challenge for you, see *All Is Well* on page 5 and do the *All Is Well* exercise on page 14.) Pay attention to your breath; let the mind be quiet and calm.

Now, very gently, bring your awareness to something that bothers or upsets you out in the world. Something or some public figure or situation that just gets under your skin. Touch the concept lightly, returning quickly to All Is Well. Breathe. Relax. Trust. Ask your guides for help. Remain open to receive guidance.

Consult your inner knowingness. Do you, personally, need to do something about this? Is it yours to do? Is there an action you could take that would make a difference? Are you pulled, or even compelled to that action? What if everything is ok just as it is? What if your job lies elsewhere at this moment?

Return to All Is Well. This can sometimes be a challenge when we are examining something with so much emotion around it. Ask your guides and non-physical support team for help. Ask if they have specific guidance for you at this point about this issue. If they do, write it down.

Return again to All Is Well. Slow your breathing; calm your mind. Let a sense of well-being and unconditional love wash over you. In this instant, everything really is ok. If something needs to be done, you will be guided to do it. If an action on your part is necessary, helpful or productive, it will rise up and demand that it be done, without you having to worry or stress. Planning might be necessary, but that will be guided as well.

Breathe slowly in and out. Take stock of your emotions. Are you ok? Agitated? Stressed? Calm? Resolved? Remind yourself that All Is Well. You have more help than you could possibly need in your guides and non-physical support team. Ask them to help you know what is best for you in this moment and around this issue.

Sometimes our guides tell us things that surprise us. Sometimes what we thought was our favorite cause or purpose is no longer appropriate in our lives. We are changing, growing, transforming, and that is just what is to be. Change *is* the constant. If we need to move beyond a favorite cause, topic, person or what we think our purpose is, it is because our unique energies are needed elsewhere. Shockingly, we sometimes need our own energy in order to make the changes that will ultimately serve our world. It is not selfish or narcissistic. It is necessary. Most of us have been conditioned to put ourselves last, if we even make it on the list. We've been told, "It is selfish to put yourself first." Self-sacrifice does not work in the New Reality. The energy is not consistent with Unity Consciousness. Old belief system, old model, old paradigm. Bye-bye!

Return to your breathing and the deep inner sense that All Is Well. If it is time to make changes in your commitments, especially to your individual self, it will be made clear. Everything does not have to be figured out and understood all at once. Small, incremental changes are the ones easiest to make and most likely to stick.

Deepen your breathing, and know that it is almost time to return to your daily life. Find the well of stillness within. Feel All Is Well in every pore of your being. Ask for help and guidance. Listen. Suspend disbelief and judgment. Let whatever your guides have to say in. All Is Well. You're ok.

Briefly and lightly, almost humorously if you can manage it, touch your attention to whatever it was you started this exercise with, that which bothered you. See if you feel differently now. It's ok if you don't. It's ok if you do. This exercise is about perception and change. Notice any differences. No judgment. Stay calm. Rein the mind in. No need for explanation. Simply notice your perceptions. Notice if anything changed.

Come back a final time to All Is Well and let that inner knowingness suffuse you. Allow it to comfort you. It's all going to be ok. All Is Well. Things can bother you. Or not. We each get to choose. Our emotional reactions will happen. We get to choose what we make that mean. Each of us. Every day. All the time.

The first few times we choose to change our perception of what is can be confusing and sometimes difficult. The old ways are so familiar. But the old ways keep us in duality and often in victim, where we feel helpless and hopeless. It is more work to choose, but it is also a lot more fun and a lot more satisfying. All points on the spectrum are valid. For example:

   "This still bothers me, but I am not going to let it ruin my day."

   "This bothers me so much that I am going to do something about it! My first step is (fill in the blank) and I'm taking it today!"

   "This concerns me, yet I can feel that it is not on my path to take it on at this time."

It's all about individual choice in the present moment, each person doing exactly what is right for them. This is how we change our world.

All Is Well. Great Job!!

Journal: Perception and Change

Journal your experience of the Perception and Change exercise. Be sure to record any messages or inspiration that you received from your inner self.

_____

_____

_____

_____

_____

_____

_____

_____

_____

_____

_____

_____

_____

_____

Journal: Perception and Change

40. Receptivity

ORACLE MESSAGE:
Stay open and receptive to Spirit's guidance as you walk your path.

What comes up for you when you consider being open and receptive to Spirit's guidance as you walk your path?

Are you spiritually receptive? What does that mean to you in this moment?

How would you describe your current level of receptiveness?

What are 3 things you can do, one of them right now, to become more receptive? To increase your receptivity?

1.

2.

3.

Ask your guides for help. Their ideas are always wonderful, and sometimes surprising!

For example, you may receive: "Have a cup of tea." *Have a cup of tea? You want me to have a cup of tea? Like, right now? That's going to make me more receptive?? A cup of tea? Really? Ok, ok, ok already! I'll have a cup of tea! Sheesh! Oh, uh, I mean thank you for the wonderful advice amazing, extraordinary guides ...*" Explore this. There is no telling what sitting down and having that cup of tea might bring.

What additional information did you receive from your guides?

Earl Grey, anyone?

41. Passion

What comes up for you when you think about letting your passion out?

What lights you up? What do you feel passionate about? A cause? A belief? Animals? People? Explore and write it here.

What have you done recently where you lost track of time? This could point to a passion.

If you could do ANYTHING, right now, what would it be?

What prevents you from living more passionately?

What steps can you take to live a more passionate life?

42. Your Inner Divinity

ORACLE MESSAGE:
*We are all the same love, the same energy expressed in a different way.
We are aligning our actions, thoughts and beliefs to support that love on this Planet.*

What comes up for you when you think about inner divinity? Do you resonate with it?

How does this message about your inner divinity align or disagree with your current belief system or faith?

What resonance would bring these concepts into balance?

What has been your experience of Oneness? Describe what it means to you.

Now, ask your guides to help you understand Oneness further. What do they say?

What can you do to fan your inner spark? What are some ideas?

What makes you feel closer to your spirituality?

What steps can you take to further birth and expand your spirituality?

43. Authenticity

What comes up for you when you think about putting yourself out there and really being authentic?

Do you feel like your True Authentic Self? Why or why not? (If your answer is that some parts do and some parts don't, give examples.)

What area of your life would you like to feel more authentic in?

Do you change yourself in any way to please others? If so, in what ways? Why?

What would it look like to be and feel and act as your True Authentic Self?

If you were to be your True Authentic Self, would anything change? How? (Lots of people say things like, "I'd lose my job," but would you really? Being true to yourself doesn't mean passing loud and hard judgments on others, or even yourself. You can be authentic and still be polite!)

What steps can you take to be more authentic?

44. Boundaries

What comes up for you when you consider putting some boundaries in place?

What do you want in your life?

What are you willing to do and not do?

Are you comfortable setting boundaries? If no, why not? If yes, what boundaries would you like to set?

Do you put the happiness and comfort of others ahead of your own? Provide examples.

What are some ways you can set boundaries to honor yourself and your personal time?

45. Strength

What comes up for you when you think about invoking strength for yourself?

Are your spiritual muscles strong? In what way?

How could you make them more so, if you wished to do that?

What spiritual practices have made you feel stronger? More balanced?

In what ways do you exercise your mental strength and stamina?

In what ways do you exercise your spiritual strength and stamina?

What in your life needs more attention and focus?

What guidance has been coming to you about it?

Are you following the guidance? Why or why not?

Do you have the spiritual strength to do what you need to do? Explain.

Where does your strength need to be right now? What can you do to build that muscle?

46. Circumspection

What comes up for you when you consider being circumspect and prudent in your life?

What in your life right now could use some circumspection or prudence? Is there a particular issue? Or several? List them here.

Are there arenas in your life where you feel like your forward progress has been blocked or slowed down?

List them here.

What adjustments need to be made, if any, in order to move forward?

What is your inner guidance telling you about these issues?

47. Life Mastery

What comes up for you when you consider the idea that life is our teacher, that every experience is an opportunity for growth?

What growth experiences are you having in your life currently?

What lessons are they teaching you?

Do you feel like your spiritual self is in charge of your life?

What parts of your life are primarily dominated by your mind?

What steps can you take to shift the authority of these parts over to your spiritual self?

What is one step you can take, in this moment, right now?

How do you think your life would change if your spiritual self, your True Self, were in charge?

What steps can you take to become more consciously aware, and to better understand, the lessons that life is teaching you?

Exercise: Transformation Checklist

This exercise presents an opportunity to check off the areas where you have made changes in your life and at the same time to make note of areas you still want to work on.

Here's how it works. Go through the list below and circle or otherwise note things you have integrated or still want to play with further. Consider using colored pens to make this list an artistic and fun planning tool. Be sure to give yourself credit. You've worked hard and made some changes.

Better idea about who I really am
Better able to express my True Self
Create quiet time
Be present
Pay attention to what IS
Let go of persons, places or things
Fired myself from ...
Fired myself up for ...
Finding my passions
Tuned in to my guides and angels
Tuned in to my own intuition
Exercise fearlessness
Built my cornerstone
Bring myself back to the present moment
Made a Gratitude List & continue to add to it
Access and listen to my inner wisdom
Bring my heart's knowingness to situations
Know and feel All Is Well
Being cautious about ...
Creating a new way of life for myself
Express appreciation
Enjoy myself and my life more
More comfortable saying no
Building community
Take more time for myself and my spiritual practices
Celebrate me and my progress!
Studied or learned about something new
Deepened relationships, including with myself
Transformed!

Journal: Transformation Checklist

What comes up for you when you review your checklist? Are you pleased with the changes you have made? Are there any other items you would add to your list? What changes would you like to make in the near future?

48. Emergence

What comes up for you when you think about allowing yourself to emerge into your new True Self?

What are some ways you feel you are changing?

What is different about you today? From a year ago? Six months? Last week?

Do you feel like your wings are growing? In what ways?

What has come forth recently from within you, that you love?

What is ready now to emerge from within you?

What are some steps you can take to help make that emergence happen?

CELEBRATE YOUR PROGRESS!!!

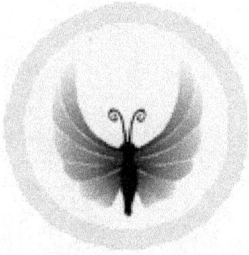

49. Connecting at the Heart Level

What comes up for you when you think about what it means to connect at the heart level?

Who have you connected with already today? This week? Was it at the heart level?

Who would you like to be able to connect with at the heart level? How can you make that happen?

Were you taught to fear strangers? Most of us were. Can you feel how this fearful conditioning has prevented us from connecting with others?

Have you overcome it? If not, do you want to? Write your feelings.

If you have already overcome this conditioning, how did you do it?

If you haven't, what steps can you take to overcome it now?

Can you sense when people or situations are not right for you? Are you able to sense or feel when things are not right? What do you do?

Do you feel any resistance to the idea of connecting with others at the heart level?

Do you feel joyful with the idea of connecting with others?

What are some ways you can connect more with others at the heart level?

50. Confidence

What comes up for you when you think about releasing your confidence? Unleashing it!

How would you describe your confidence level?

Has your confidence level changed recently? In what way?

What would help you to feel more confident, right here, right now?

Are you aware of your own spiritual power? Describe your power.

Are you walking your own path with confidence, ready to stand alone if need be?

Do you trust in yourself no matter what is happening?

Do you feel like you are always in the right place at the right time?

What steps can you take to increase your confidence?

In what areas of your life do you most express your confidence?

What steps can you take to ground your confidence and more fully express it in your life?

51. Alignment

ORACLE MESSAGE:
*We need to constantly remind ourselves, minute by minute,
to stay grounded and aligned no matter what is going on.*

What comes up for you when you consider consciously aligning yourself with your Divine Essence?

What is your life's purpose? Do you know what it is or have some idea of what it might be? Describe anything you know about it, if you do. Ask your guides for help.

Do you feel aligned with your purpose? Are you living it? Give examples.

What helps you to stay balanced and aligned?

How did it feel when you did the ball of light exercise in the book *You Can Transform Your Life*? What came up? Did you see or feel anything? Did a vision arise? Describe your experience.

List at least 3 activities that you can easily add to your daily experience to support your alignment.

1.

2.

3.

52. Transformation

What comes up for you when you consider your transformation?

How can you liberate yourself as much as possible from old ideas, old habits, old relationships and old patterns of thinking? Ask your guides.

What areas of your life have you intentionally transformed already?

What areas of your life are currently in the process of transformation?

What areas of your life have you been hesitant to transform? Why?

List your favorite spiritual practices that support your ongoing changes.

If you could completely transform one area of your life in an instant, what would it be?

Do it! Begin the transformation process! Make a plan. You have the skills, the experience, the energy and the support to do or change whatever you choose!

Describe the new way of life that you are ready to embrace:

Congratulations! You have completed *You Can Transform Your Life ~ Go Deeper!*

ORACLE MESSAGE:
*Transformation is a truly worthwhile purpose and goal.
The end result is the evolution of consciousness.*

In whatever manner you have been using these tools, exercises and practices, you have reached the book's conclusion ... however, there really is no conclusion. Transformation and its processes continue throughout our lives as we integrate what we have learned and applied into our everyday life. It is an ongoing evolution of our very own consciousness. Concluding this part of your journey is something you can be very proud of. Celebrate your commitment and your success!

Now it is time to focus on the specifics that will support you as you move on into your future. Review the changes you have considered or the changes you have made to your life. This is a benchmark opportunity to see how far you've come. Go you!

What has transformed in your life since beginning the *You Can Transform Your Life* book and the *You Can Transform Your Life ~ Go Deeper* workbook?

What has been your greatest transformation?

What have been your greatest challenges or obstacles?

How did you overcome these challenges or what steps are you taking to overcome them?

What practices from *You Can Transform Your Life* have been your favorites?

Which practices will you continue to use to support your ongoing changes?

What plans do you have for future transformation?

What's next on your journey?

How will you celebrate YOU?

Be kind to yourself! Appreciate yourself! Celebrate YOU!

YOU'VE COME A LONG WAY!!!

**Your True Self is shining through and is filled with
the unique sovereignty that belongs only to YOU!**

CONGRATULATIONS!!!

© 2013 Lotus Wisdom Publishing

Love and Trust, my dear ones ... Love and Trust!

GRATITUDE AND APPRECIATION

Darity Wesley

The creation of this workbook was a complete and spontaneous outgrowth of the *You Can Transform Your Life* book. Guided and directed by our guides and angels, we strongly felt that there was a need to Go Deeper in the process of transformation with the *You Can Transform Your Life* book. It was all about moving the tools, the practices, and the process to an expansion of experience for you, the reader. So many readers were supporting this next step in the process, so thank you for your encouragement. You are all loved and supported from here to there.

I wish to thank Melissa Morgan and Paula Wansley for all the hard work and energy they have put into this companion guide, *You Can Transform Your Life ~ Go Deeper.* They are amazing women and I love them both so very much.

Melissa Morgan

It has been an honor and a privilege to work with both Darity and Paula on *You Can Transform Your Life* and the *You Can Transform Your Life ~ Go Deeper* workbook. The power of the practices, tools and information has made a huge impact on my life and personal journey. From the founding of our personal law editing team of Finicky, Snickedy and Snilly to the hilarity of endless ellipses, we have had a marvelous time.

Transformation is rewarding, deep and powerful work. Taking it to the next level, going deeper, as it were, is a reflection of the depths of Darity's wisdom, insight and inspiration. I personally plan to work with these materials for the rest and my life. I am exceedingly grateful to have the opportunity. And speaking of gratitude, I would not have been involved in any of these works without the life-long friendship of my brilliant and extraordinary friend, Cristina Smith.

I salute the courageous readers who have taken on the challenge and gone deeper.

Paula Wansley

I wish to thank Darity Wesley for providing me with the opportunity to work side-by-side with her on this extraordinary journey of *You Can Transform Your Life* and the *You Can Transform Your Life ~ Go Deeper* workbook. Her continuous love, support and encouragement have had a significant impact on my life. It is an honor to know her, to be friends with her, and to be able to support her as she shares her love and wisdom with the world. She has become such a bright and beautiful light in my life and I am so very grateful to be able to share this grand adventure with her. What a ride! Wheeee!

I also very much appreciate Melissa Morgan, and her delightful editing team of Finicky, Snickedy and Snilly. LOL! She has a remarkable eye for editing detail which I very much appreciate (being a perfectionist, myself). It was a pleasure sharing this *You Can Transform Your Life* journey with her. Many laughs, a few sneers, and much sweet camaraderie.

I also wish to thank Cristina Smith, beautiful soul, for guiding me to Darity, and for all of the other amazing opportunities she's offered to me over the years. Her kindness has expanded my world and continues to be an impetus for the expression of my creativity, skills and passion. I am filled with gratitude and appreciation.

Lastly, I would like to acknowledge my precious daughter, Taylor, whom I love so very much. I am so grateful to have her in my life and cherish her more than words could ever say. ♥

ABOUT THE AUTHORS

Darity Wesley

Darity Wesley, award winning author, lawyer, speaker, Death Diva and Modern Day Oracle experiences life to its fullest. A long time traveler on the spiritual, metaphysical, esoteric and personal development path, Darity has transformed her life many times in many ways.

Having concluded a fabulous 35 year legal career as a privacy and information security guru and business lawyer, Darity has now transitioned into focusing full time on the *Modern Day Oracle™ Wisdom Teaching Series.* She is inspired to share all of her favorite tips and tools of transformation that she has learned along the way.

Darity has provided her *Modern Day Oracle™* messages since 2006 to subscribers all around the world. If you would like to join the *Modern Day Oracle™* community, please visit our website and subscribe!

www.DarityWesley.com

If you would like to contact Darity, please send an email to Darity@DarityWesley.com

Paula Wansley

Paula Wansley is an artist, freelance virtual business support provider and subtle energy intuitive.

Paula has many hats in her freelance career closet, including web design, graphic design, creative consulting, photography, video editing, self-publishing assistance, professional editing, software instruction, internet research, book-keeping and general small business assistance. She is also a legal assistant and award-winning motivational speaker.

If you would like to contact Paula, please send an email to pwans333@gmail.com or visit www.paulawansley.com

Melissa Morgan

She's always been a little different. When not editing, Melissa Morgan is a harpist, composer, teacher, writer and crystal healer. She loves music, rocks, words and books.

Melissa's harp recordings are genre breaking, from New Age to Celtic, Classical to jazz, with Space Harp in between. Her current project is a series of magical children's books and interactive musical performances that are the adventures of Blue Mermaid™. A symbol of flow, self-love and compassion, Blue Mermaid™ teaches acceptance of self at the deepest level. Featuring the jewelry and related stones of Blue Mermaid™, which started as a piece of music, Melissa's sites include:

www.etsy.com/shop/MyBlueMermaid
www.etsy.com/shop/HealingRocks
www.HealingRocks.info
www.mmmHarp.com

If you would like to contact Melissa, please send an email to mmharp@gmail.com

Transformation is about stepping more and more into

becoming your best and most authentic self.

When you consciously stand in the truth of who you *really* are,

you truly find balance, happiness, fulfillment.

These things come from being who you are ... who you REALLY are.

What you need, what you want, who you are ... all come from within.

~ Darity Wesley

Also by Darity Wesley

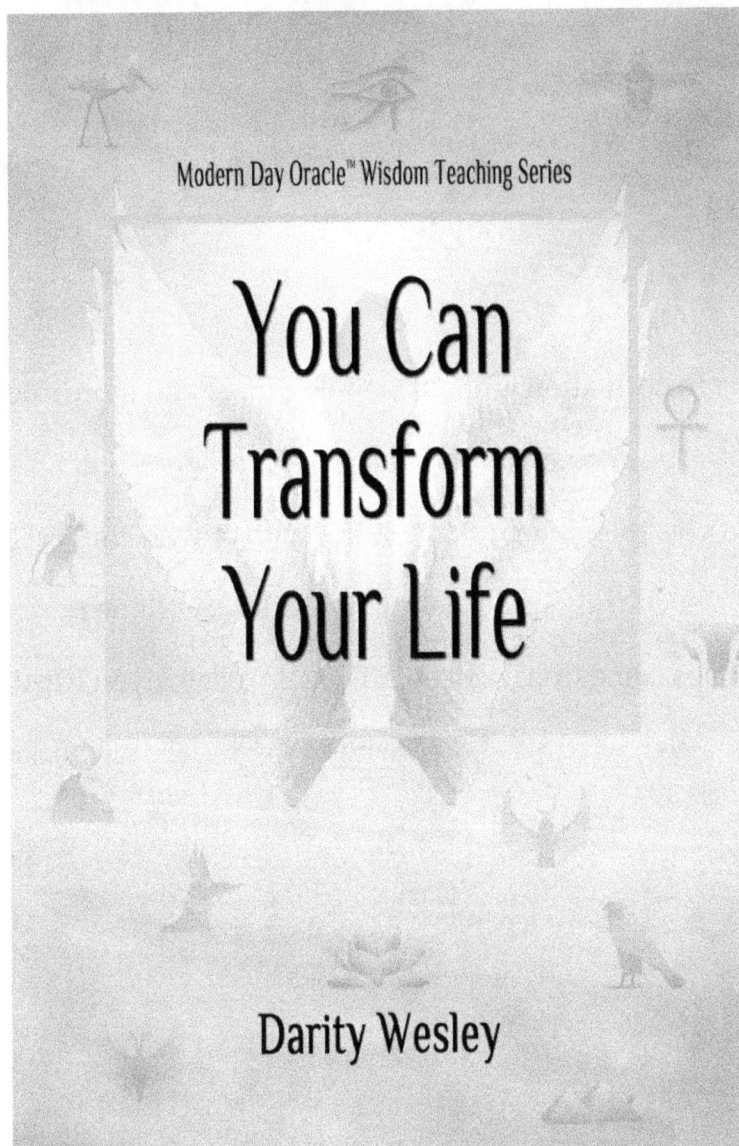

Modern Day Oracle™ Wisdom Teaching Series

You Can Transform Your Life

Darity Wesley

YOU CAN TRANSFORM YOUR LIFE

by Darity Wesley

Have you ever dreamed of making changes to your life ...
to feel more in harmony with yourself and your world?

Have you ever wished you could express your true potential ...
to live a life that expresses who you really are?

Have you ever wanted to increase your intuition ...
to communicate with your Higher Self, Guides and Angels?

If so ... You Can Transform Your Life provides a way!

You Can Transform Your Life provides processes, tools and practices to take you on a journey of transformation. Offers a simple step-by-step plan to support you every step of the way!

Contains 52 Oracle messages of inspiration, affirmation mantras and symbols, with practical tips and tools for deep inner transformation, leading you along the path of self-discovery and to new levels of awareness.

You Can Transform Your Life provides a plan that can help support and guide you on a journey of personal growth and spiritual transformation.

Modern Day
ORACLE

Modern Day Oracle™ Wisdom Teaching Series - Book 1

ISBN 978-0-9995425-07

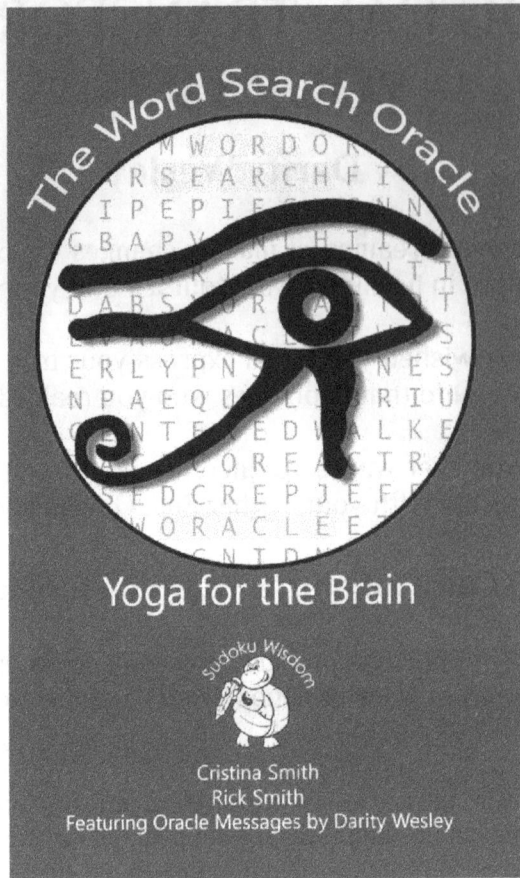

The Word Search Oracle

Yoga for the Brain

Sudoku Wisdom

Cristina Smith
Rick Smith
Featuring Oracle Messages by Darity Wesley

Winner 2017 Pinnacle Achievement Award
Games and Puzzles

THE WORD SEARCH ORACLE
Yoga for the Brain™

**Featuring Modern Day Oracle™
messages by Darity Wesley!**

Every puzzle is both a challenge to be solved
and a meditation for self-realization.

Filled with fascinating facts and
enlightening insights.

Enjoy 60 fun-filled word search puzzles
each with a hidden Oracle message!

Have fun with a purpose!

The Word Search Oracle
Invites You to Play!

ISBN 978-1544211558

www.ingramcontent.com/pod-product-compliance
Lightning Source LLC
Chambersburg PA
CBHW080935040426
42443CB00015B/3418